Pebble® Plus

Your Senses at the Dentist's Office

by Kimberly M. Hutmacher

Consulting Editor: Gail Saunders-Smith, PhD

CAPSTONE PRESS

a capstone imprint

Pebble Plus is published by Capstone Press,
151 Good Counsel Drive, P.O. Box 669, Mankato, Minnesota 56002.
www.capstonepub.com

Books published by Capstone Press are manufactured with paper
containing at least 10 percent post-consumer waste.

Library of Congress Cataloging-in-Publication Data
Hutmacher, Kimberly.
  Your senses at the dentist's office / by Kimberly M. Hutmacher.
    p. cm.—(Pebble plus. Out and about with your senses)
  Includes bibliographical references and index.
  Summary: "Simple text and full-color photographs describe using the five senses at the dentist's office"—Provided by
publisher.
  ISBN 978-1-4296-6664-0 (library binding)
  1. Dentistry—Juvenile literature. 2. Teeth—Care and hygiene—Juvenile literature. 3. Senses and sensation—Juvenile
literature. I. Title.
  RK63.H88 2012
  617.6—dc22   2010053938

Editorial Credits
Erika L. Shores, editor; Veronica Correia, designer; Svetlana Zhurkin, media researcher;
    Laura Manthe, production specialist

Photo Credits
All photographs by Capstone Studio/Karon Dubke, except cover background by Shuttersock/Creations

Note to Parents and Teachers

The Out and About with Your Senses series supports national standards related to life science.
This book describes and illustrates using the five senses at the dentist's office. The images support
early readers in understanding the text. The repetition of words and phrases helps early readers
learn new words. This book also introduces early readers to subject-specific vocabulary words,
which are defined in the Glossary section. Early readers may need assistance to read some words
and to use the Table of Contents, Glossary, Read More, Internet Sites, and Index sections of
the book.

Printed in the United States of America in North Mankato, Minnesota.
032011   006110CGF11

Table of Contents

Off to the Dentist!

Where do we go to keep
our teeth clean and healthy?
That's right! Today we will
use our five senses
at the dentist's office.

What We See

Look around.

Magazines cover tables.

See the TV. Now it's time

to go to the exam room.

A bright light hangs

above the big chair.

Shiny silver tools sit on a tray.

What else do you see

in the room?

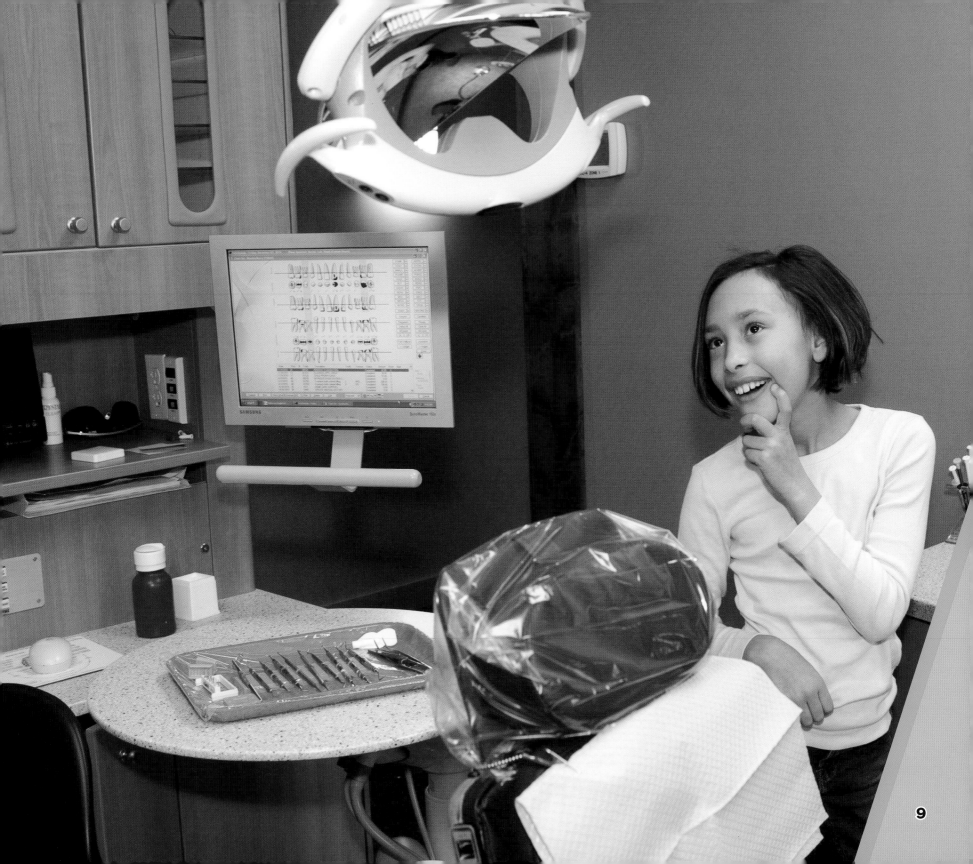

What We Touch

Feel the bumpy paper napkin

covering your shirt.

The hygienist's gloves

feel smooth.

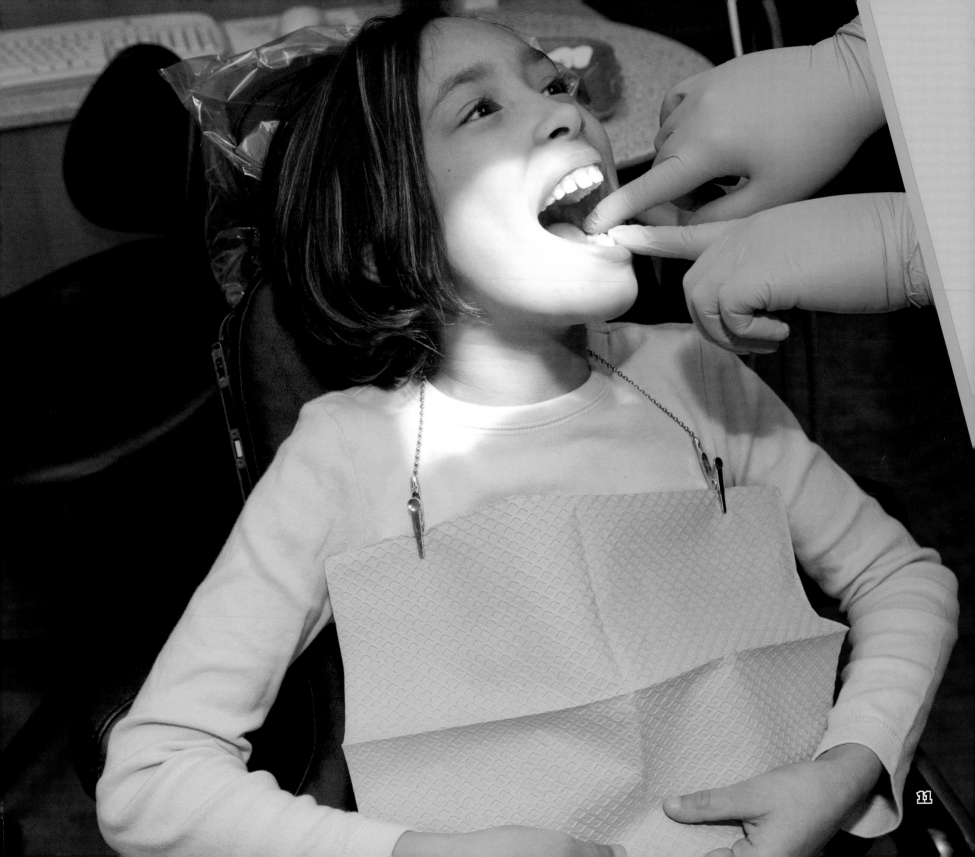

A tooth polisher spins
and tickles as it cleans.
The polish feels gritty
on your tongue.

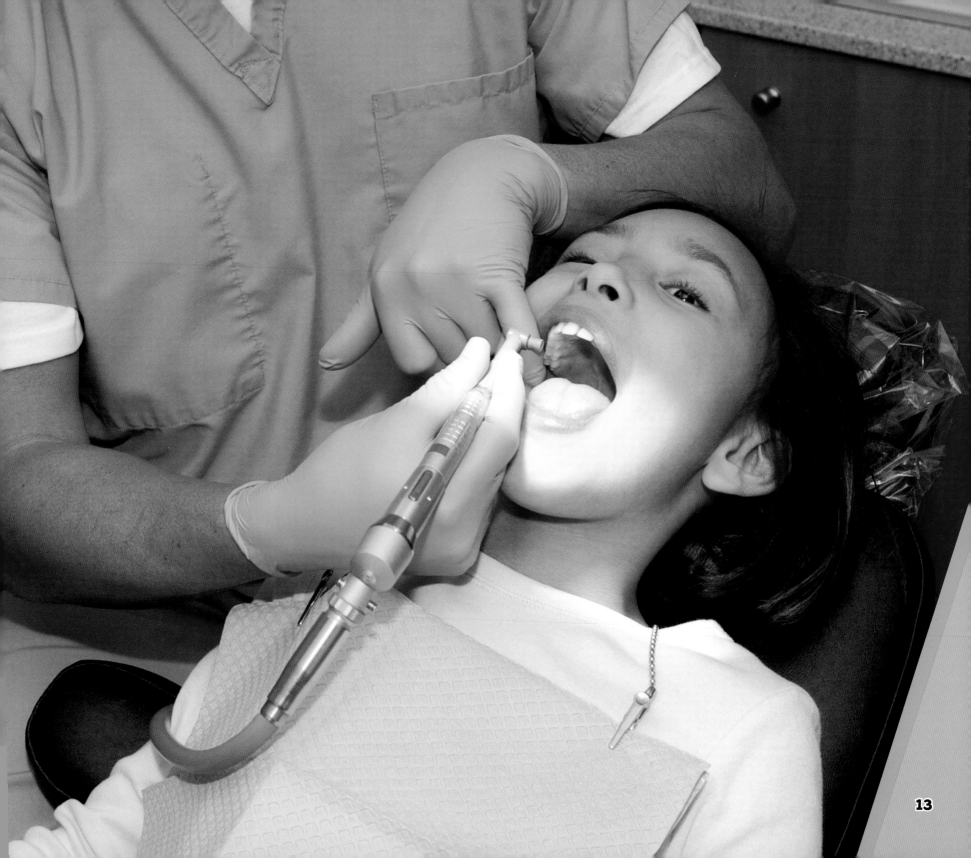

What We Smell

Sniff, sniff. The smell of
disinfectant fills the air.
The exam room and tools
are kept clean and free of germs.

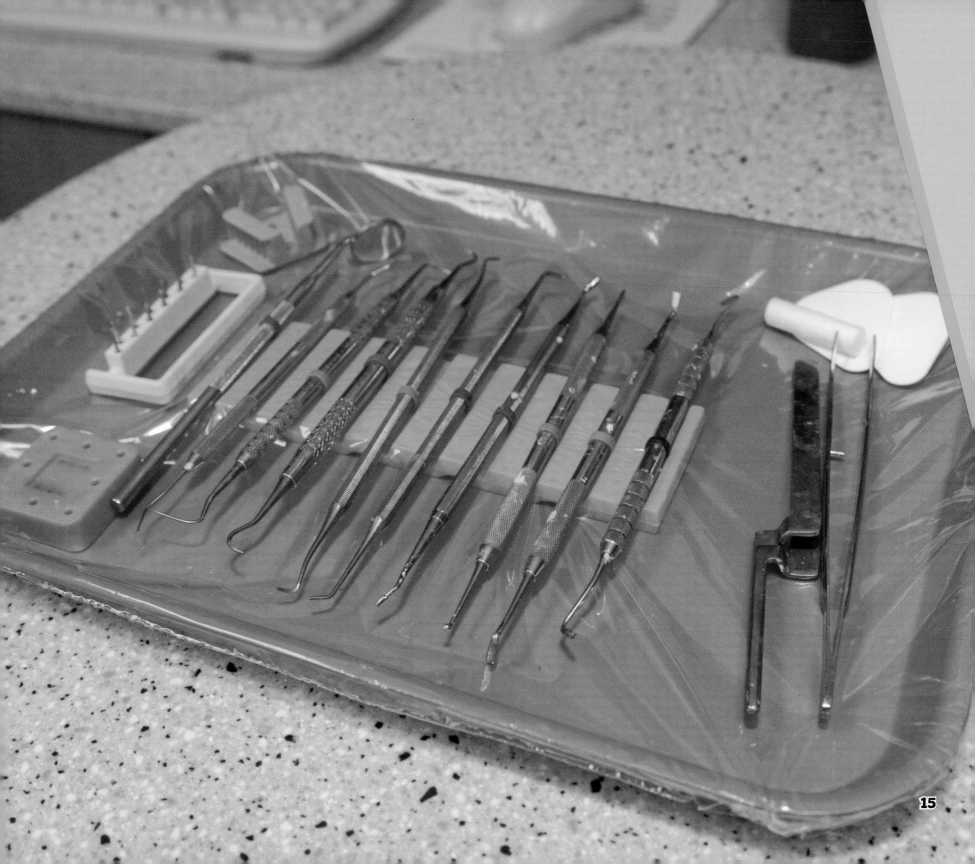

What We Hear

Whir, whir! The drill makes

a buzzing sound.

Soft music comes

from a speaker.

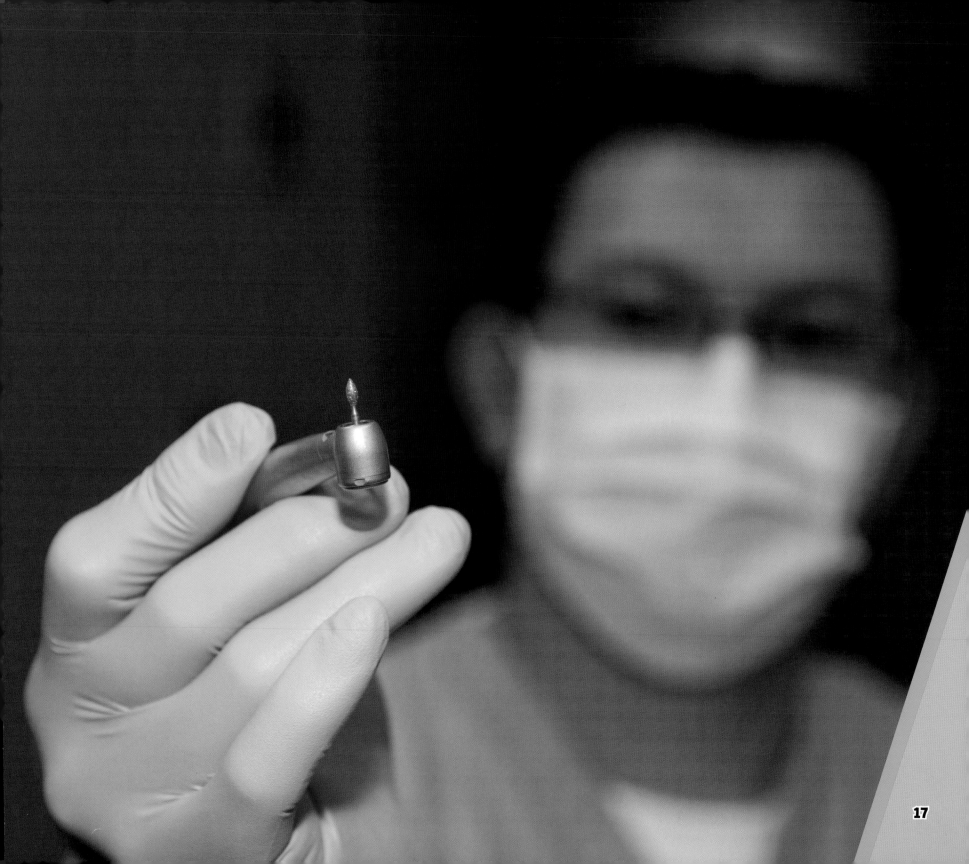

Listen. Gurgle, gurgle.

The saliva ejector sucks up

saliva and water

from your mouth.

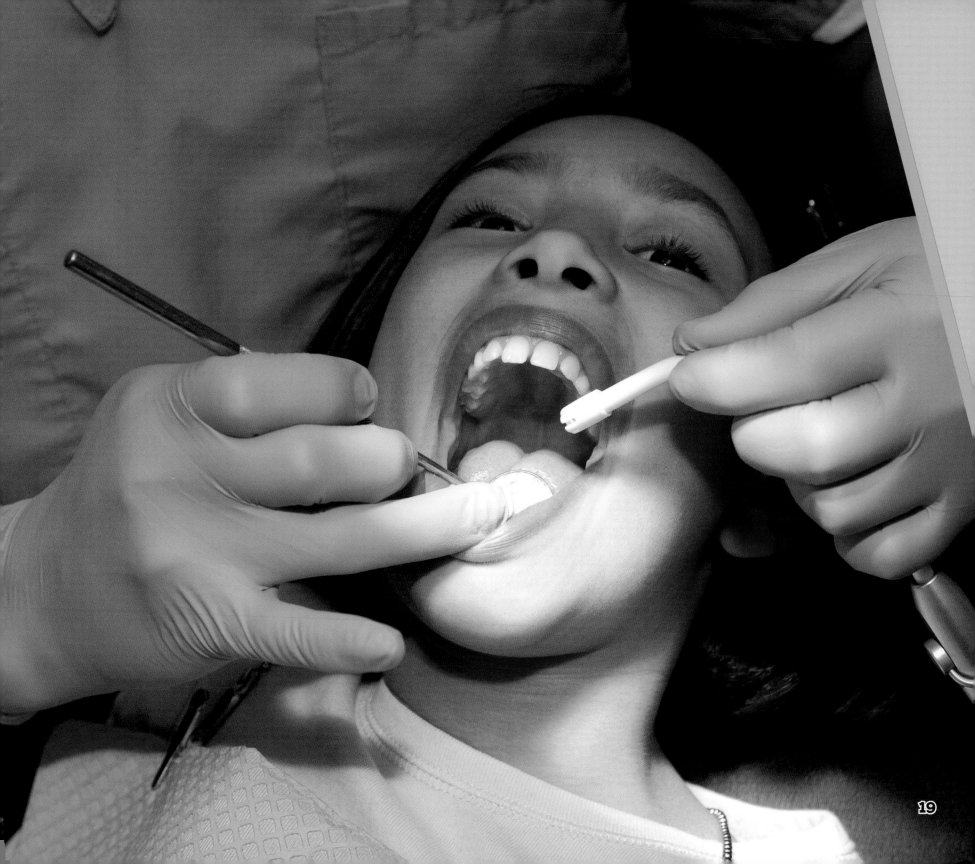

What We Taste

Our trip ends by using our sense of taste. Mouth rinse tastes minty. We'll take home bubble-gum flavored toothpaste to keep our teeth clean.

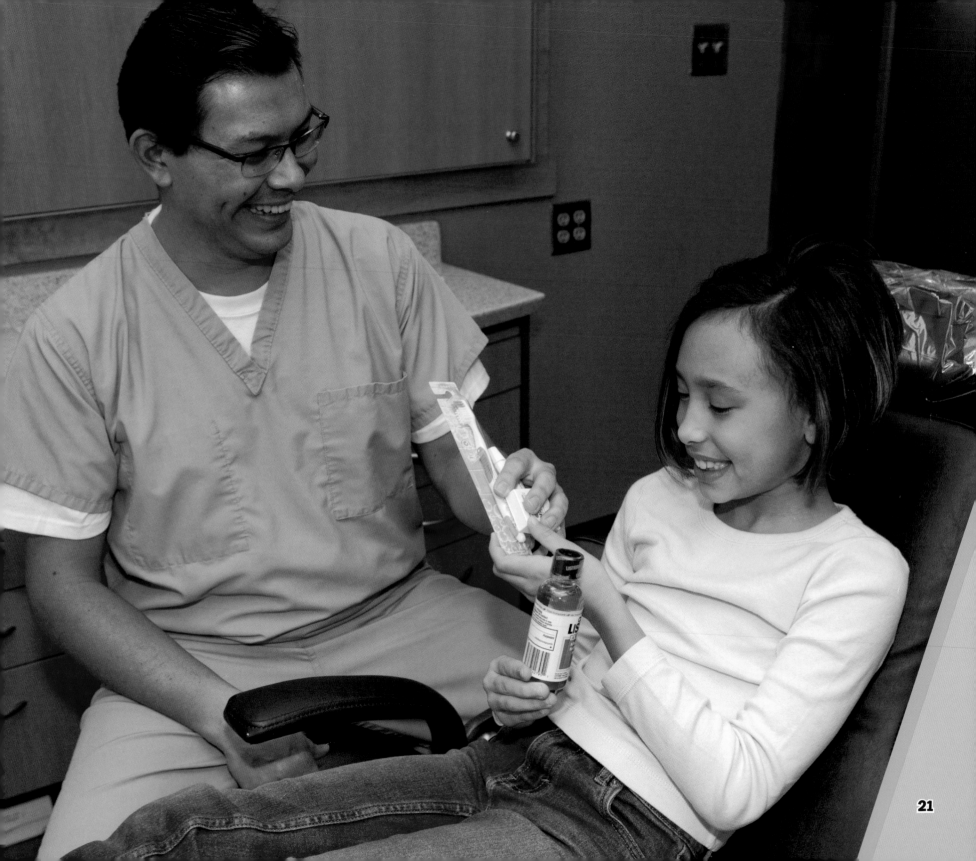

Glossary

disinfectant—a chemical cleaner used to kill germs

germ—a very small living organism that can cause disease

hygienist—a person trained to clean teeth

saliva—watery fluid in mouths

saliva ejector—a tool used to suck saliva and water out of the mouth

sense—a way of knowing about your surroundings; hearing, smelling, touching, tasting, and seeing are the five senses

Read More

Crabtree, Marc. *Meet My Neighbor, the Dentist.* Meet My Neighbor. New York: Crabtree Pub., 2010.

Feldman, Jean, and Holly Karapetkova. *Five Senses.* Vero Beach, Fla.: Rourke Pub. LLC, 2010.

Kalman, Bobbie. *My Senses Help Me.* My World. St. Catharines, Ont.; New York: Crabtree Pub., 2010.

Internet Sites

FactHound offers a safe, fun way to find Internet sites related to this book. All of the sites on FactHound have been researched by our staff.

Here's all you do:

Visit *www.facthound.com*

Type in this code: 9781429666640

Super-cool stuff! Check out projects, games and lots more at **www.capstonekids.com**

Index

Word Count: 166

Grade: 1

Early-Intervention Level: 16